Things I'd Tell Myself

Dawn Gates

BookLeaf Publishing

India | USA | UK

Presentation by *BookLeaf Publishing*

Web: www.bookleafpub.com

E-mail: info@bookleafpub.com

ISBN: 9789360946982

First edition 2024

Things I'd Tell Myself If Only I Would Listen

Stop eating
like the next meal isn't coming
You haven't been there
in a while
Stop loving
like you don't deserve nothing
Give yourself a reason
to smile
Take pride
in every gift you're giving
No one else can
do it like you
Don't give up
on the things worth keeping
Appreciate every

day that is new
You are built
for ages beyond
Don't settle for the status quo
there is no
right or wrong
Just lessons
to help you grow
You are more
than the image in the mirror
Her reflection merely a shell
Your promise
is not in your beauty
But in the depths
of an untapped well
Remember
your soldier spirit
It reminds you
of your force
But don't let it overpower
your unassuming voice
You are the gift
of legends
Despite your mortal pain
The secret builds
within you
Your time has come to reign

Try Hard

There are no easy answers
I love like life's gonna end
That's why I take my chances
I don't hold back, I jump right in
Probably should play much smarter
But when it comes to my heart
That's when I fight much harder
Because soon it all falls apart

I'm not a romantic
So much as I'm real
It could all blow up
So let's make a deal
Surrender to me
I'll surrender to you
If we both let go
We could see it through

No matter the cost
No matter the pain
I'll stand there with you
Through sun and through rain
My love carries on
Even if you're not game
I've suffered before
I know I will again

First

First
There is the release
Then the omigod
Here we go again
How much longer
Until we are no longer friends
Next
Comes the worry
The wait, the weariness
Aren't you, are you
Will you
I'm wearing my love like a
Shoe that can be discarded
Quickly
Or worn in from overuse
Then
You say the things
That fill me

Then leave me in starving pain
Like a water hose shower
Abruptly shut off
Just as I adapt to the pressure
Finally
I succumb, I'm numb
Bruised and aware
That this is the love
My love is willing to share

This Time

I broke my first rule
I got used to you
I got attached
Can't get that back
I broke my own heart
Right from the start
When I gave it away
When I let you stay
Over and over I go
The cycle remains unbroke
What have I done this time

I love pain
I love the way it tastes
Touching my skin
Running down my face
I love hurt
No one can do it worse
Fall on my knees
Pleasure the curse
Why am I so crazed
Unstable, unfazed
Have I come undone
Since I lost the sun
I'm dead and walking

I'm mute and talking
The matrix won't take
I'm my own mistake
Over and over I go
The circle is still unbroken
What can I do this time

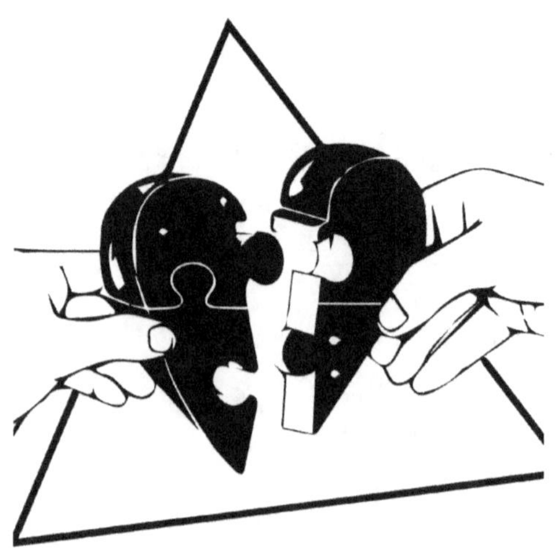

Token

I will not be your token
After words left unspoken
Left you fragile, weak, and weary
I can't stand to see you near me
I'm confused by how you act
Like a wounded bird attacked
After words you chose to spew
Seemed to overpower you
Go ahead and play that role
Let the darkness eat your soul
You cannot have mine to gloat
As you sink down in the moat
Look up high, my castle stone
Impenetrable to your words thrown
I will not be your token
I will not be yours broken

The Birth

The day I met you
I met me too
One of us expanding
the other brand new
I couldn't know then
How much I would love you
Because when you were born
I gave birth to me too

The Commute

I swore I'd never live in Maryland again
The terrain of cars churning out smoke, anger,
And weariness grates on my soul
Making each venture
an exercise in the art of not
breaking down
I spot debris in the construction-laden lane
And wince as barriers block my view
of the immovable force that's keeping
me frozen for the moment
Frozen moments leading to wandering thoughts
It's not the state that bothers me,
Although the persistent building and
rebuilding of more spaces to accommodate
the dozens of denizens traipsing each square
mile
is excessive
More will come, more will go
and the trees will wilt and recede in time,
It's the memories that I've stowed away in the
trunk, thoughts of times good and bad,
loss and love, hate and pain
that persist in my rearview
just out of view but lingering
Is that the same debris from before?

Stuck in place while stuck in places
that I keep returning to
Should I hold out hope that this road
will be finished soon, that I'll drive out
to find many open lanes, clear for miles?
Will I keep driving the same route
in spite of the destination
seeming further and further away?

We Have A House

We have a house
Walls, doors, and steps
Pictures to prove
We belong here
Lights that flicker and fade
While dust multiplies by the day
Stuff to store our stuff
And furnishings to hold us up
And down
We have dishes, stains, and leaks
Spaces yet explored
Seasons on display
We have floors that bear our marks
Chips and dents
The spot where the painting fell
And scored the wall black
We have chairs climbed
To unlock the back door
A quick escape by socked feet
On pale wood
Little wheels race against
The carpeted floor in search
Of the darkness the couch provides
We have raised voices
In tension and love

Angry sighs and playful pinches
A lightness towards hope
In a dark-filled realm
We have a house
And we make it a home

Winter's End

I'm awash with the mist
Of early dew
As I sit by the lake
And think of you

As I gaze overhead
At the murky sky
I remember the
Newness of days gone by

Fresh evergreen
The trees start to turn
But the ache in my chest
Gives way to burn

Moist drops fall
Beneath my cheek
And stain the water
With a rippled streak

I sway with grief
My heart heavy weighs
Wishing the reflection
Reflected in gray

The sunlight bursts
As clouds abate
Spring comes alive
Winter seeking out its sate

Get Up

Fists bared, knuckles scraped
Lift and lift
And drop until the blood courses through
Your muscles, glowing in your skin like
Chem lights in a dark forest
Hustle, tussle
Ignore the wet grass
Plastered to your face
Push, push
Harder until you
Are the only one left to
Rise

The Bird

It cries and I rush
To soothe and calm
The morning light
Just touching the edge of the window
It calms and we settle
And we wait for the day to start

It cries and I dawdle
Waiting just a while longer
For the afternoon haze
To dissipate
I arrive just as the whimpers
Cease and the rays
Lull us both into a slumber

It cries and I do nothing
But let the twilight seep
Through window cracks
It cries and so do I

Mourning the day
The peace has fallen
And we're both consumed
By the dark

Dream

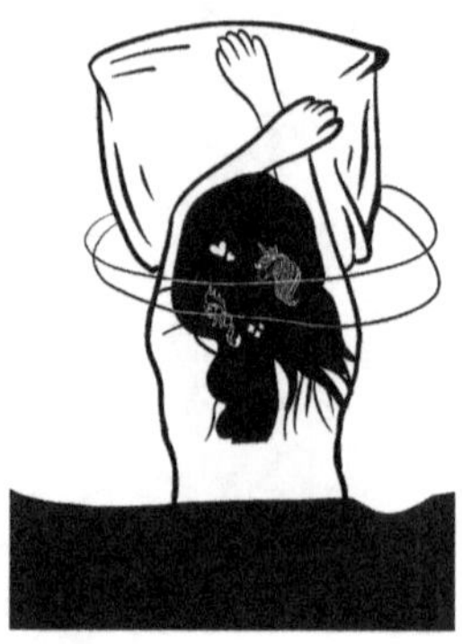

You are not
My dream come true
In my wildest dreams
I could never imagine you
You're the depth
Of my soul
I have yet to breach
You're the air in the shadows
I can never reach
I could search
For eternity and
Never find you
While you wait in my pocket
Just slightly out of view
I am torn with love
For your heart I can't win
But you give it generously
Even now, even then

Fears

I'm scared I'll die
Before seeing your face
I'm scared I won't be a good mother
I'm scared you'll never know how much I love
you
I'm scared of failing you
I'm scared you'll never come back
I'm scared you'll die too soon
I'm scared you'll blame me
I'm scared I'll never be worthy of that pedestal
I never thought I'd get this far
I'm scared it will all disappear

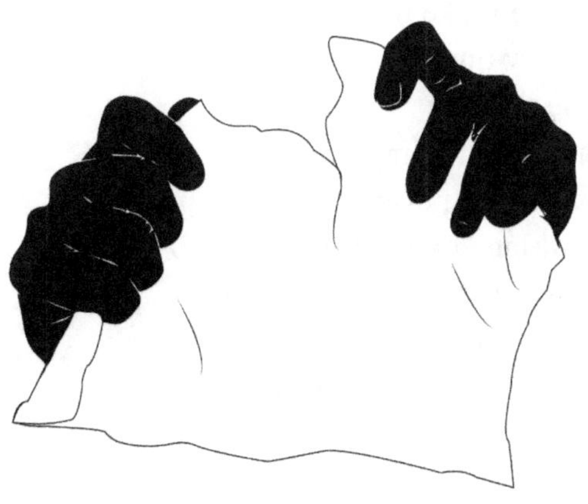

Avoid Sanity

You take me for a ride
One I never thought I could survive
Up down side to side
And yet I've never been more in love
I shouldn't take the time
But every time you call
I come running
I must be out of my mind
Because I've never been more in love
Everything you do drives me crazy
I should walk away but I won't
Because deep down you're mine
You're the only one I want

Almost

Almost got through the day
Without wondering if you're ok
Almost made it to girls' night out
Without calling the house
Almost erased from my head
All the loving things you said
Almost made it through another day
Almost
But then I remember
All the memories
Like back in November
When we were at ease
The love that we had
I know it was real
But now I remember
What I'm not supposed to feel

Ocean Blue

The waters clear
Shallow and rippling
My toes dripping with
Cool sand
A postcard view only
Made better
Because you were right there with me

Parking

I rush to park
But not because I'm eager to work
I just hate trekking from far away
Into the gray old building
I park and paint
My face, my hair twisted
Into intricate ropes
Atop my head
Sometimes forethought
And sometimes the improvised
Is better
I rush to park
To mitigate
The winter and cold
The rain and soggy
I contemplate my options

If I rise up the ranks
And get an assigned spot
How delusional
To aspire to greatness
Just to get a closer
Parking spot

What I Need

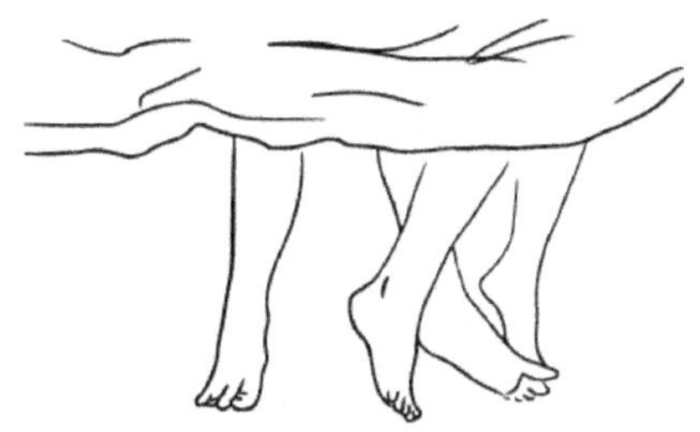

I want your body
don't want your pain
might see you tomorrow
or never again
If you see the sun
you've been here too long
don't care if it's right
don't care if it's wrong
It's just what I need

Don't want to worry
don't want to fuss
don't want a future
because there's no us
just want a feeling
from the inside out
no complications
no fears, no doubts
It's just what I need

Corinthi-Ends

It's not the love that ends
But the trust that wanes
and the softness that fades
In the looks of despair
And the fear is raised
Through long-wound days
And frothy nights that
Leave you sweaty and spent
But empty and lost
The reset never takes
And you're left lonely
Not alone
It's not the love that ends
But the friendliness
The gratitude and understanding

The willingness and grace
That used to envelop
Every word uttered
It's the longing of yesterday
Competing with the weariness
Of today
It's the old me
Wrestling with the reality
Of present me

Path

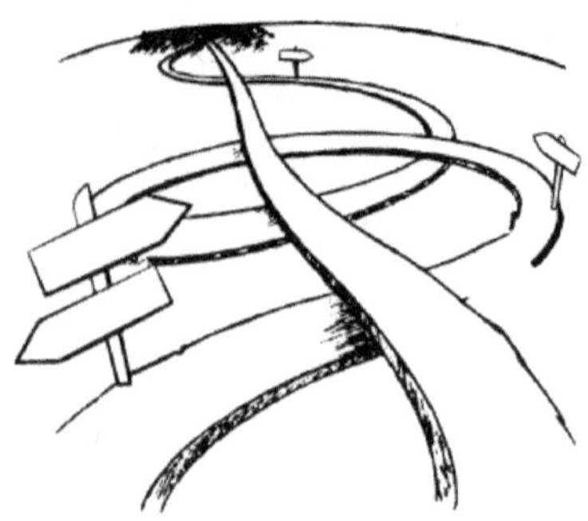

There's more than one way
And yours doesn't always
Have to be the hardest
There's more than one day
And yours doesn't always
Have to be the darkest
There's a time to be strong
And a time to be light
And a time to be cold
And a time to be bright
Those things that comfort you
Are as permissible
As the things that make you
Steel, strong, and solid
It's easy to hold on
In survival mode

It's easy to forget
That you can choose
Your path

Dawn

At the clearest part of day
When the light breaks just so
And the wind is still
And the clouds are
Like shedding cotton
Losing their thread
I ascend, gathering momentum
With each flicker of light
Each ray pulsating through me
I rise above, hovering,
Protecting with a warmth
And caress akin
To a strong embrace
My advance is slow but
Encompassing
My manner simple
Yet powerful

I graze through the world
Ever present and invisible
I am there
I am Dawn